MW01676241

Church Programs for Special Days

Compiled by
Elaina Meyers

Standard® PUBLISHING
Bringing The Word to Life
Cincinnati, Ohio

Editorial team: Elaina Meyers, Rosemary H. Mitchell, Courtney Rice
Cover design: Brigid Naglich
Inside design: Edward Willis Group, Inc.

Published by Standard Publishing
Cincinnati, Ohio
www.standardpub.com

ISBN 978-0-7847-2263-3

Contents

Celebrate throughout the year! This book contains easy-to-use material to help churches plan services for 10 special days!

In the Face of Change

DIANNE MCINTOSH

Summary: QUIRK learns the simple truth that having the remedy for a messed-up life but not applying it does no good.

Characters:

SCRIPTURE READER—reads Scripture at the beginning and end of the skit
QUIRK—ghastly-looking person (male or female) who is seeking a change
LIFTER—pleasant-looking person (male or female) who knows how to obtain lasting change

Setting: street corner, anywhere
Set: 2 chairs center stage with backs facing audience
Props: fake warts, warty nose, stuffing for humped back, ratty wig, 2 pocket-sized identical jars
Running Time: 5 minutes

SCRIPTURE READER: "Do not merely listen to the word, and so deceive yourselves. Do what it says. Anyone who listens to the word but does not do what it says is like a man who looks at his face in a mirror and, after looking at himself, goes away and immediately forgets what he looks like. But the man who looks intently into the perfect law that gives freedom, and continues to do this, not forgetting what he has heard, but doing it—he will be blessed in what he does" (James 1:22-25, NIV).

[QUIRK is standing alone, talking to self. QUIRK has warts on his face, a large warty nose, humped back, ratty hair, and one leg that appears shorter than the other. He is holding a small jar.]

QUIRK: Boy, do I feel terrible. Everything's gotten worse this year! Wow! I'm a mess. I don't understand why.

[LIFTER walks cautiously up to QUIRK who has a sickened facial expression.]

LIFTER: *[disbelief]* Quirk? Is that you?

QUIRK: *[gruffly]* Yeah, it's me. Who do you think it is?

LIFTER: You look . . . um . . . different.

QUIRK: You mean I look terrible.

LIFTER: Frightening, really.

QUIRK: Well, don't beat around the bush about it.

LIFTER: Sorry, I mean you look so . . . well, . . . so . . .

QUIRK: I'm a mess. I've got these big warts that won't go away. My back is humped over. One leg has grown longer than the other, and my hair is turning into a rat's nest. Plus I feel scared all the time, like something really awful is about to happen.

LIFTER: *[aside]* I think the "something really awful" already did happen. *[to QUIRK]* Wow, you are a mess. How long have you felt like this?

QUIRK: *[discouraged]* A long, long time. It keeps getting worse. This year I've got to find a way to change.

LIFTER: You're right! The new year is just the right time for a change.

QUIRK: Do you have any suggestions?

LIFTER: Let me see . . . what's that jar in your hands?

QUIRK: Oh this? *[holds up jar]* It's called Peace and Healing Cream. You're supposed to use it daily on your face, arms, legs, and torso in order to ward off warts, humped back, unwanted leg growth, hair problems, and rotten feelings that something awful is about to happen.

LIFTER: Have you used it?

QUIRK: *[defensively]* I've been carrying it around for years, and it doesn't seem to do any good.

LIFTER: But have you applied it?

QUIRK: You mean have I put it on my face, arms, legs, and torso?

LIFTER: Right. Have you used the cream on yourself?

QUIRK: Not exactly. In fact I really thought just carrying it around would do the trick. It's hard work to rub this stuff on. Plus, what if I go to all the trouble of applying it and it doesn't work?

LIFTER: Quirk! What are you talking about? Why carry it around if you won't even try it for yourself? I happen to know that it does work. Look here. *[pulls out a jar of the same cream from pocket]* I have a jar of the same stuff. The difference between mine and yours is that I apply mine.

QUIRK: Well, I'll be. That's amazing. I always wondered why you didn't have trouble with warts, humped back, unwanted leg growth, and ominous feelings of awfulness. Here all this time I thought I was so smart to have the jar. I thought just toting it around would be enough. I never thought of actually following the directions and using the stuff.

LIFTER: Give it a try and let's see what happens.

QUIRK: OK if you think it might work. . . . I guess I'm ready to try anything.

[Quirk opens the jar and begins rubbing the cream onto his body. A transformation occurs. As Quirk applies the cream the warts drop off, the warty nose falls off, hump back slips away, legs become the same length, and the ratty wig falls off. Quirk stands up straight and smiles.]

Quirk: *[excited]* Look at me! I'm a new person!

Lifter: *[nods head sagely and smiles]* So you are. You see it really does work if you do what it says. But Quirk, please use it every day.

Quirk: Oh, I will! I couldn't bear to look at that awful face in the mirror again. This stuff is wonderful! Who would have thought a person just needed to follow the directions? This year is truly going to be a new year!

Scripture Reader: "Do not merely listen to the word, and so deceive yourselves. Do what it says. Anyone who listens to the word but does not do what it says is like a man who looks at his face in a mirror and, after looking at himself, goes away and immediately forgets what he looks like. But the man who looks intently into the perfect law that gives freedom, and continues to do this, not forgetting what he has heard, but doing it—he will be blessed in what he does" (James 1:22-25, NIV).

New Year's Poems

TIME

MARSHA CHUDY

1 Year
12 Months
52 Weeks
365 Days
8760 Hours
525,600 Minutes
31,536,000 Seconds
31,536,000,000,000,000 Nanoseconds
Time . . . One year . . . What will you do with it?

NEW YEAR'S PRAYER

SALLY JADLOW

The year stands before me as an empty page—
a clean slate of hours and days.

My Lord, make me wise with the time You've given.
Show me those I may direct to Heaven.

Fill my heart with Your purity
and open my eyes to see as You see.

Where there is hurt, bring Your healing;
in confusion, grant Your revealing.

To those on life's ash-heap,
use me to apply Your relief.

When I look back and this year is done,
may I rejoice in the walk I've had with Your Son.

MY WISH FOR YOU

LOIS ROTZ

I have a New Year's wish for you
to brighten all your way,
a wish that God will bless you
and guide you every day.

Each month, each week, each day, each hour
may peace and joy abide,
as Christ in love and tenderness
walks closely by your side.

2009 IS HERE

LOIS ROTZ

Ring out the old, ring in the new,
2009 is finally here.
And we with hope and hearts so glad
look forward to this brand new year.

God only knows what lies ahead
in the coming months and days;
but this we know without a doubt,
He'll be there with us all the way.

MY THOUGHTS ON RESOLUTIONS

LOIS ROTZ

"What's a resolution?"
I asked my mom one day.
"It's a promise to be good," she said
and then she walked away.

I thought and thought, then thought some more.
What could I ever do
to make a resolution? 'Cause
I'd have to keep it too.

And being good is awful hard
for a little child, you see.
And so I have decided
resolutions aren't for me!

A NEW YEAR'S EVE REWIND

DOUGLAS RAYMOND ROSE

Instead of going to lots of parties,
here's a goal for which we should strive.
Rewind what we've done the previous year—
stop and take stock of our lives.

Have we managed to "love one another"
and always carried out the Golden Rule?
Have we been faithful in our worship,
utilizing all of our talents as tools?

Have we respected the elderly and children?
Helped the poor and immigrants survive?
I wonder would this new year be different,
if we stopped to take stock of our lives?

THE NEW YEAR

DOLORES STEGER

So joyously the new year starts,
the hope of peace rests in our hearts;
our resolutions, may they be
God-centered and kept faithfully.

A NEW DAWN

DOLORES STEGER

Regrets and misfortunes,
cast them aside,
let God bear the worries you fear;
today's a new dawn,
just as He planned,
the dawn of a joyous new year.

NEW YEAR'S COMING

KAREN M. LEET

New Year's coming,
New Year's here,
full of promise
loud and clear.
Full of hopes and
full of dreams,
full of plans and
crazy schemes.
Full of peace and
joy and love,
full of blessings
from above.
New Year's coming,
New Year's here,
full of God
who's always near.

A NEW YEAR CREED

DOUGLAS RAYMOND ROSE

As I face another new year,
I harbor no fears you see.
If God cares for cattle on 1,000 hills,
I know He cares for me.

As I face another new year,
His tender mercies I see.
If God cares for each little sparrow,
then I'm sure He cares for me.

Martin Luther King Jr. Is Free

IRIS GRAY DOWLING

Summary: Mom and Dad invite a surprise dinner guest to celebrate Martin Luther King Jr.'s birthday (January 15, 1929). They review memories of his life.

Characters:

Ethan
Emily
Mom
Dad
Martin Luther King Jr.—(impersonator)

Setting: family room
Props: costume for impersonator
Transition Music: "We Shall Overcome," C.A. Findley
Running Time: 5 minutes

Children arrive from school and meet Mom who is in working clothes.

Children: Hi, Mom. Why are you dressed like that?

Mom: I want you to straighten your rooms.

Children: Why today?

Mom: We're having a dinner guest.

Ethan: Who's coming?

Mom: It's a surprise.

Emily: I don't like surprises.

Mom: You'll like this person.

Ethan: How do you know?

Mom: He's famous.

Emily: Give us a hint, please-s-s-e.

Mom: Then it wouldn't be a surprise.

Ethan: Does Dad know who it is?

Mom: Yes. He's happy to have this guest.

Ethan: I think I'll call him.

Mom: No, not at work! He won't tell you anyway.

Ethan: He might give me a hint.

MOM: You're wrong. Now get busy. You don't want this guest to see your mess, do you?

ETHAN: Come on, Emily. Let's go.

[CHILDREN exit.]

[Transition Music]

[CHILDREN enter.]

ETHAN: We're done. Will you give us a hint now?

MOM: You wrote a school report about him.

ETHAN: I wrote lots of reports, but at least we know it's a man.

MOM: *[smiles]* Yes. He had a wife and four children.

EMILY: What else?

MOM: He was born in Georgia. He went to colleges at Morehouse, Crozer, and Boston University.

ETHAN: I know! Do you, Emily?

EMILY: I need more hints.

MOM: His grandfather sharecropped. His parents preached.

EMILY: Did he follow them?

MOM: Maybe.

ETHAN: How could we have the guest I'm thinking about? He's not alive.

MOM: What makes you say that?

ETHAN: He was shot in 1968.

MOM: Right, but he's alive because he knew Jesus as his Savior.

ETHAN: He's in Heaven. How can he be our guest?

MOM: Remember, it's a surprise. Let's review more before he comes.

ETHAN: Since I wrote the report, I know he tried to get equality for all people by teaching nonviolence.

MOM: Yes, he taught peaceful ways, but sometimes things got a little rough and people twisted his words.

ETHAN: In my research, I learned his life was threatened several times and he was put in prison.

MOM: He couldn't control evil in the hearts of others, but he tried promoting peace and self-control with his followers.

ETHAN: He started the Southern Christian Leadership Conference to cooperate with other religious leaders.

MOM: They marched against racial discrimination and for voting rights for black people.

Emily: I know who you mean now! Look what I found in this book. In 1963 he led 200,000 people to march from the Washington monument to the Lincoln Memorial. Then gave a speech saying these famous words: "I have a Dream that one day this nation will . . . live out . . . its creed . . . that all men are created equal."

Mom: He continued to talk about the dream. He talked and wrote five books based on biblical ideas. Some people got impatient with his slow, peaceful methods.

Ethan: Dr. King decided more people needed equal rights.

Emily: What people do you mean?

Ethan: Poor Appalachians, Native Americans, and Hispanics weren't being treated fairly.

Mom: They planned the "Poor People's March" on Washington in 1968.

Ethan: Maybe we could sing the song the marchers made famous: "We Shall Overcome."

Mom: That's a good idea. Let's practice.

[Use any instrument; Mom sings with Children.]

[Transition Music]

Mom: I think we're ready for Dad to help greet our guest.

Dad: *[knock]* Hi, everyone. *[hugs Mom and Children]* Are we ready for our guest?

Ethan: Sure . . . when's he coming?

Dad: Very soon.

Emily: *[knock]* The guest is here.

Mlk: Hello, I heard about a family who prepared dinner in my honor. Is this the house?

Ethan: Yes! Please come in. We'd like to hear why you kept working for other people's rights when you got persecuted and mistreated.

Mlk: I had to suffer and march with the others if we wanted to gain anything. It wasn't easy to work for this dream of equality and justice.

Ethan: But you won the famous Nobel Peace Prize.

Mlk: Yes, but the dream didn't get accomplished right away.

Emily: At least the prize committee recognized your peaceful efforts.

Mlk: I wanted all people everywhere to be able to say with me: "Free at last, free at last, thank God Almighty, I'm free at last."

Dad: But they can.

Mlk: Yes, if they accept Jesus as their Savior from sins they'll have freedom which puts them on Heaven's path.

Dad: You're right, Dr. King. All people need to know there is no real freedom until they reach Heaven's shores.

Mom: Let's have dinner. Then we can talk more with our guest.

Ethan: Who are you really? Martin Luther King hasn't come back to life yet, even though we know he will when the trumpets sound for our march into Heaven.

Mlk: That's a good observation, son. Let's say I'm a person who likes to keep Dr. King's ideas and memories alive. Now let's enjoy our dinner together.

[Music as all exit.]

A Prayer for Martin Luther King Jr. Day

EVA JULIUSON

Heavenly Father,

I remember as a child admiring Dr. Martin Luther King Jr. He was a dreamer, a visionary, a man after Your own heart. I believe You gave him a crystal-clear vision of Your children of all races, nationalities, and denominations playing and worshiping together. Dr. King longed to help bring that vision about in a peaceful manner during very turbulent times. I remember being shocked and deeply saddened when he was shot and killed for trying to help bring this dream about.

Father, he is now living the dream, isn't he? You give all of us a peek at the vision when You tell how there will be those from every tribe and every nation who have been bought with Jesus' blood and they will be united in love in one kingdom! Your kingdom!

Father, use me to help bring about this same vision of all kinds of people joining Your kingdom. Some day all Your children will play, eat, live, and love together! Use me to help bring about Your kingdom here on earth as it is in Heaven! Use me to make the dream come true! In Jesus' name, amen.

Martin Luther King Jr. Day Poems

MARTIN LUTHER KING JR.

IRIS GRAY DOWLING

In the middle of the twentieth century
lived a man named Martin Luther King.
He wanted justice and equality
so that everyone in this land could sing.
Whether rich or poor, or black or white,
he longed to hear the words: "Let freedom ring!"

THE MARCHER

DOLORES STEGER

Who's that marcher there I see,
walking tall and peacefully,
striving for equality?

Who's that marcher with a dream,
whose visions some may call extreme,
though justifiable they seem?

Who's that marcher with a will
to build a city on a hill
and noble promises to fulfill?

Who's that marcher looking so?
From Heaven's realm he looks below
and asks mankind God's love to show.

THAT MAN

DOLORES STEGER

There he is; it is that man,
he's speaking to the crowds;
he talks about a dream he has,
a message clear and loud.
His hope is that equality
throughout the land may bring
the world to a togetherness
that's wished for by this "king."

THE MAN

DOLORES STEGER

The man cried out, "Equality
and justice; set my people free;
God's love binds all humanity."
May all the world this truth now see.

ODE TO AN AMERICAN HERO

DOUGLAS RAYMOND ROSE

Leaders come and leaders go,
but few their praises people sing.
The exception to this American rule
is Dr. Martin Luther King.

Leaders often soon sink into sunsets.
Few heroes like Washington remain;
but God bless this historic exception:
Dr. Martin Luther King.

A SALUTE TO MARTIN LUTHER KING JR.

DOUGLAS RAYMOND ROSE

There are few with greater vision
than Dr. Martin Luther King;
to our world he brought a star—
the hope of peace to us did bring.

There are streets named after him.
In his honor, holiday choirs sing.
That is why on this special day,
we salute you, Dr. King.

The Lullaby

NANCY B. GIBBS

Summary: MEREDITH is the mother of the bride. While listening to her daughter say her wedding vows, MEREDITH's mind wanders back 23 years earlier. She was unmarried, pregnant, and planning to have an abortion. Then MEREDITH met someone and her life was completely changed.

Characters:

MEREDITH—mother of the bride
LISA—a young mother-to-be who is pro-life
NURSE

Setting: hospital waiting room
Props: 2 chairs, child-care magazine, 2 baby dolls, red rose, lullaby instrumental music, file folder
Running Time: 20 minutes

SCENE 1

MEREDITH steps onto the stage.

MEREDITH: We have all heard the saying, "Always a bridesmaid; never a bride." This has been true for me for more years than I can remember. But today, I sat on a special seat. I was honored as the mother of the bride. I watched as my only daughter married a very special young man. I was never married, you see. Yet at an early age, I became a mother. I had decided to terminate my pregnancy. But then I met Lisa. She too was an expectant mother. We were both sitting in a hospital waiting room. We were both three months pregnant. Lisa was bubbling over with excitement. I was overwhelmingly frightened. Lisa was waiting to have an ultrasound. She was so happy. I was waiting to have an abortion. I didn't think I could raise a child by myself.

[LISA walks in, sits in a chair, and begins to read a child-care magazine. MEREDITH sits down beside her.]

LISA: *[looks up from her magazine]* Hi, I'm Lisa.

MEREDITH: I'm Meredith.

[A lullaby is played over the loudspeaker.]

LISA: Do you know what that means, Meredith? *[MEREDITH shakes her head.]* The playing of a lullaby means a baby was just born. Isn't that exciting?

Meredith: Sure.

Lisa: I'm here to have a sonogram. *[rubs her tummy]* What are you here for?

Meredith: I'm here to talk to someone about having an abortion.

Lisa: Oh no. So there will never be a lullaby played for your baby? Are you sure? You know your baby does have a right to live and to have a lullaby played just for him or her.

Meredith: It's not exactly what I want, but I have no choice. I have no husband, I don't have a job, and I cannot support a child.

Lisa: God will help you. *[Meredith stares at the floor.]* Could I pray with you?

[Lisa takes Meredith's hand.]

Lisa: *[prayerfully]* Dear God, please help Meredith and her baby. Meredith is feeling hopeless right now, Lord. Give her the strength to carry the baby full term and give her what she needs to raise to raise this child. Amen.

[About that time a second lullaby plays. Meredith begins to cry. A nurse walks into the waiting room holding a chart.]

Nurse: Lisa, come on back. The doctor is ready to see you.

[Lisa hugs Meredith and both ladies leave the stage in opposite directions.]

Lisa: *[speaks from backstage]* I have to hurry to tell Meredith I am having a boy. *[Lisa walks back onto the stage and straight toward the chair where Meredith had been sitting. She cries.]* I wonder if Meredith went through with the abortion. *[Lisa leaves stage notably upset.]*

SCENE 2

Five months later. Lisa steps back onstage (in pajamas, holding a baby). Meredith walks in from the opposite side of the stage (also holding a baby).

Meredith: Oh, hi, Lisa. Do you remember me?

Lisa: Sure I do . . . I have thought about you often since we met.

Meredith: Thank you for your prayers, Lisa. You saved my child's life. It was you and the lullaby that changed my mind about having the abortion. That's the reason I have my baby today. And of course, God had a lot to do with it too. He has answered so many of my prayers.

Lisa: I am so happy, Meredith. I had worried about you and the baby.

[The ladies look at each other's babies. They hug. Both ladies leave the stage.]

SCENE 3

Meredith: *[walks back in and addresses the audience. She is holding a red rose.]* It's been 23 years since that day. My daughter just handed me this red rose. She and her groom said their wedding vows at the altar today. Then she took her husband's arm and started toward the back door. On her way out, however, she stopped and handed Lisa a red rose from her bouquet. Little did Lisa know the day she prayed for my unborn child that she was praying for her future daughter-in-law! God really does see the big picture! Regardless of the difficulties giving birth to a child can bring, especially for a single mother, my daughter has brought me more joy and happiness than any other earthly thing I have ever had. Many times, as I watched my child grow up, I thanked God for Lisa and for the lullaby that played in the hospital that day. Every child has the right to live and the right to have a lullaby played just for her. And every young lady has the right to walk down an aisle, arm in arm with the man she loves. How could any loving mother take the right to live away from her child?

I Hear You Whisper

KAREN M. LEET

Hidden deep within me, life so new I can hardly believe you are real, and yet your presence touches me and fills me with wonder. I study myself in the mirror and I am more than only me now—I am also you. My body is your home, your protection, your safe place.

From your earliest moments, I am aware of your dependence on me. It's my job to provide for you—who else could do it? My choices affect you. My actions carry you along with me. I am living for two now—living not just for me, but also for you.

Every day when I wake, my first thoughts are of you. How are you? What is happening with you? I think of your growth, how your body and mind form within me. How you change and thrive. As I move through my days, I think more and more of you and the amazing miracle of new life inside me.

I read books to learn more and see pamphlets from the doctor. I watch videos and take classes. I shop carefully to meet your needs, and I work hard at this new job of mine—becoming your mom, the best mom I can be.

And, above all else, I pray. I thank God for you, little one—I thank Him for entrusting you to me. I thank Him for every moment of your life. I praise Him for the wonder of it, the miracle of it, the joy of it. I pour out my hopes and fears, my concerns and dreams. I ask for His protection for you, His blessing, and His guidance for your life. I pray that you will love Him as I do, that you will give your life to Him and spend your days with Him.

I sit and rock. I sing worship to God as I clasp my arms around my body, around you, and we are together, we three—my child, myself, and my God. No words can hold the feelings surging through me, and I lift wordless prayer to Him.

Some moments as I plan and pray, as I wait for your birth, I wonder. How can anyone not see? How can anyone not feel, not think, not realize? From the first moment, you were there—real and alive, your entire life before you—created by God, entrusted to me, an astounding event, a new person.

I bow my head in painful prayer for those who do not understand, who feel anger or fear or indifference and refuse the life within them. I cradle you, blessed baby. I feel you leap inside me and feel my own heart leap in response.

And when I listen carefully, I hear you whisper, "I love you, Mommy." I smile and nod. Then I whisper in return, "I love you too, little one. I love you too."

Sanctity of Life Poems

THE AUTHOR

DOLORES STEGER

First, He formed an outline
and a plot devised,
filled it in with details,
then He scrutinized
each line very carefully,
marked off chapters too,
built up to a climax,
suspenseful, bold, and new.
He crafted out an ending
with which He reconciled
a marvelous beginning:
His work He titled "Child."

SACRAMENT OF CHILDHOOD

DOUGLAS RAYMOND ROSE

Come sense the sacrament of childhood
in the spirit of a small child,
leading us back from worldly things,
back to the face of God.

Come tap the sacrament of childhood,
become again as a little child,
regain divine fellowship with Him,
born in a manger, meek and mild.

God sends us dear sons and daughters.
He gives them most generously
to lead us gently back to Him.
His face all the better to see.

A LITTLE CHILD SHALL LEAD THEM

(BASED ON ISAIAH 11:6)

DOUGLAS RAYMOND ROSE

Thank God for all the little children—
with them we are beautifully blessed;
they paint our life with excitement
and frame it best with zest.

Thank God for all the lovely children
sent straight from our Father above;
they fill our hearts with happiness
and warm us with their love.

A GARDEN OF CHILDREN

DOUGLAS RAYMOND ROSE

The home is like a fresh garden.
Our children sprout as sweet vines.
They grow like special plants of love—
around our hearts entwined.

Our love is like the warm sunshine.
We water our offspring with tears.
We're proud of our garden of children.
God bless them all through the years.

ODE TO SANCTITY OF LIFE

DOUGLAS RAYMOND ROSE

Life is surely so sacred
from the cradle to the tomb;
God has known us all
from our own mother's womb.

The world has enough problems
without us adding to life's strife;
that's why we hold so sacred
the sanctity of life.

THE LOVING OPTION

DOUGLAS RAYMOND ROSE

Our daughter wouldn't be here
and neither would our son—
for if they had been aborted
we would not have either one.

Our children are both adopted
from mothers who thought ahead;
they sacrificed their own feelings
so their dear children could be safely led.

We thank God for our sweet children.
We've given them love and our own name;
they grew not under our hearts—
but in them just the same.

Momma's Boy

JOHN COSPER

Summary: A biker's tattoo causes two unlikely men to get into a discussion about what a blessing moms can be.

Characters:

Chains—a biker
Dale—an accountant

Setting: bus stop
Props: cell phone
Running Time: 5 minutes

Chains is standing at a bus stop. He is a stereotypical biker with a skull tattoo on one arm and a heart with the word MOM *on the other. Dale walks up. He sees the heart tattoo and starts to giggle. He tries to hide it, but Chains notices.*

Chains: What?

Dale: I didn't say anything.

Chains: Somethin' funny?

Dale: No, not at all.

Chains: Sure seems like it.

Dale: I'm sorry. I don't mean to be . . . I just noticed your tattoo.

Chains: What about it?

Dale: Just seems a little funny. You know?

Chains: In what way is it funny?

Dale: Well, you're obviously a tough guy. Probably ride bikes. Belong to a gang.

Chains: So?

Dale: Come on. You have a heart that says "Mom."

Chains: You don't have a tattoo like this one?

Dale: Of course not.

Chains: And why not?

Dale: Because I'm not—no, forget it.

Chains: You're not what?

Dale: No, forget it. I don't want to die.

Chains: I grant you immunity. Now spill!

Dale: I'm not a . . . Momma's Boy.

Chains: MOMMA'S BOY???

Dale: Please don't kill me!

Chains: Kill you? For that? It ain't worth it.

Dale: Really?

Chains: You think you hurt my feelings callin' me a Momma's Boy? Let me tell you something. I'm proud to be a Momma's Boy! And any jerk who isn't a Momma's Boy . . . well, I just feel sorry for him.

Dale: Why?

Chains: Because Momma's the one who brought you up!

Dale: So?

Chains: So? Just think where you would be if Momma weren't there. When you fell out of a tree and got a boo-boo, whose kiss made it all better?

Dale: Mom's?

Chains: That's right, Mom's! When you went to school and you opened your Fonzie lunch box, who was it that packed your lunch?

Dale: Mom?

Chains: That's right—Mom! Who was it that took you to soccer practice and piano lessons?

Dale: You took piano lessons?

Chains: That's right, I took 'em! Momma drove me every week and came to every recital. You know why?

Dale: You scared her too?

Chains: Because she loved me.

Dale: Right, my bad.

Chains: But it wasn't just that. It was the little things that made my Momma special. The way she cut my peanut butter sandwiches into a heart. The way she winked at me when I actually got a C+ on my report card. The way she listened and was so tender when my first girlfriend Medusa ran off with that other guy. *[sniff]* I'm sorry. I just really miss my mom.

Dale: I'm so sorry. Did she die?

Chains: She's doing a nickel for assaulting a police officer. But she's out in May, and I don't know about you, but I can't wait to hug my Momma again.

Dale: Wow, I . . . I'm really sorry. I didn't realize your Mom meant so much.

Chains: Yeah. It breaks my heart so many people take their Ma for granted. Maybe everybody should have their Mom locked up. Might make 'em appreciate them more. *[sniffs]* Sorry. I gotta got find a tissue or something.

[CHAINS walks off. DALE pulls out his cell phone.]

DALE: Hi, Mom? It's me, Dale. . . . No, nothing's wrong. No, I don't need money. I just wanted to tell you . . . I love you. Thanks for being so great.

Mother's Day Poems

MY MAMA'S LOVE

DOUGLAS RAYMOND ROSE

I brought my mama old feathers.
She gave to me warm hugs.
She kissed my forehead sweetly
when all I gave her were bugs.
I brought my mama rocks of treasures.
She gave her all to me—
she counts me her boyish treasure.
Mama means all the world to me.

A MOTHER'S DREAM

DOUGLAS RAYMOND ROSE

Mother had a dream for me,
She planted it in love—
she watered with her tears
and prayed to God above.

Mother had a dream for me.
She encouraged me every day.
She said I could do anything,
if I my course did stay.

Her dream is filled with wonder.
I've come a long, long way;
Mother had a dream for me—
that's why I'm here today!

I LOVE YOU, MOM

LORENA E. WORLEIN

I love you, Mom, so very much.
I may not always show
the deep affection that I have,
but I want you to know.
You really mean a lot to me.
Mere words could not express
my gratitude for all you do,
the many ways you bless.

You've taught me many needful things
and been there at my side
to nurture and to care for me,
to lead me and to guide.
Of all the mothers in the world
you are the very best.
Without a doubt you are the one
I'd choose over all the rest.

So, Mom, I want to honor you
not just on Mother's Day
but on each day throughout the year,
and so I humbly pray,
"Dear Lord, help me to show my love
in all I say and do."
Dear Mom, I truly want to be
a blessing unto you.

THOUGHTS OF MOTHER

LENORA MCWHORTER

My life is full of meaning
because of my mother's care.
I have many sweet memories
of her always being there.

Mom introduced me to Jesus
and asked Him to save my soul.
She lives the Christian life
like no one else I know.

Mother delights in helping others
with her special, gentle touch.
Always reaching out in love
and shares whether little or much.

No one is as special as mother.
So very bright is her light.
She is a model for everyone
on how to live upright.

Mother leaves a trail behind her
of love and faithfulness
and a path for us to follow
because she gives her very best.

My mom's faith is evident.
She is always ready to forgive.
You know she walks with Jesus
because of how she lives.

A MOTHER GIVES THANKS

DOUGLAS RAYMOND ROSE

I love you, darling daughter.
I also love my fine son.
Although you are both adopted,
we've all bonded into one.

We all are born-again believers.
Our Father God guides us each day;
we're part of the great family of God.
We have received Christ's own DNA.

I thank God for you, dear children.
I've loved you dearly from the start.
Although you didn't grow under it,
you grew fast within my heart.

MUSINGS ABOUT MY DEAR MOTHER

DOUGLAS RAYMOND ROSE

Marvelous, her cheerful words
Obvious, her sacred smile
There never was a single day
Her hands paused to rest a while
Each deed she did was special
Right and truth were her marquee

That's why Mother's Day is special.
God made my mom just for me!

THE GIFT OF LOVE

DOLORES STEGER

Mothers are like packages,
I do believe it's so.
Each is a different size and shape.
Each has a different glow.
In one way, though, they're all alike,
give thanks to God above.
In each one of these packages,
He placed the gift of love.

A GODLY MOTHER

DOUGLAS RAYMOND ROSE

She caresses the baby at her knee.
She prays over him like no other—
nothing is more loving and wonderful
than the love of a godly mother.

She watches and protects him.
Her theme is "Love one another."
Nothing is more awe-inspiring
than the love of a godly mother.

MY MOM

AMY HOUTS

I love the way you look at me,
as if you like just what you see.
And when you take my hand in yours,
I feel so safe, like nothing more
in this wide world could bother me
or make me sad. I'm worry-free.
I hope one day that I can be
a mommy, just like you are to me.

MAMA'S PRAYER

DOUGLAS RAYMOND ROSE

Her door was open—just ajar.
I saw her kneeling there.
And I couldn't help but overhear
Mama say my name in prayer.

Now she's gone away to Heaven.
No more can I see her praying there.
But whenever I face another problem
I still hear her say my name in prayer.

Why We Fight

JOHN COSPER

Summary: The spirit of a World War II soldier shows up at an antiwar protest and reminds everyone that it was men like him who selflessly sacrificed for the USA that gave them the right to protest.

Characters:

Mick—an outdoor war protest
Joe—spirit of a World War II soldier
Protesters

Setting: recreation room at a ski lodge two days before Christmas
Props: picket signs, megaphone, World War II soldier gear
Running Time: 5 minutes

Mick leads a crowd of antiwar Protesters on stage, chanting. The crowd quiets for Mick to speak.

Mick: For too long this government has shipped our young men and women off to die for its own greedy gain.

Crowd: Yeah!

Mick: It's time we stand up to them!

Crowd: Yeah!

Mick: No more blood for oil!

Crowd: Yeah!

Mick: No more dying for old rich men!

Crowd: Yeah!

[Joe enters, listening.]

Mick: Our children are dying in a foreign country. It's not my country, and it's not my fight.

Crowd: No!

Mick: Do you want to die for people half a world away?

Crowd: No!

Mick: Do you want your children to die for total strangers?

Crowd: No!

Mick: Then call your senators! Call your representatives! Call the president and tell them to bring our kids home!

[Mick sees Joe.]

Mick: There's one right there. Look at him. So young, so full of promise. The government wants to ship him off and put him in the line of fire.

Crowd: Booo!

Mick: Are we going to let this young man die?

Crowd: No!

Mick: Come on up here, buddy. Tell the people who you are.

Joe: My name is Joe Cooper from Columbus, Ohio. I was born in 1924 and drafted into the service in 1942 to fight the Germans.

[The Crowd mutters.]

Mick: Is this a joke?

Joe: No, sir. I was a proud member of the D-Day invasion force. I gave my life saving a friend on the beach at Normandy. I'm proud to stand here before you today as a man who served my country.

Mick: A man used by his country.

Crowd: Yeah!

Joe: On the contrary. Back in my day, we still believed in things like defending the weak and combating tyranny. Our freedom came at a steep price, and we were willing to die to ensure that freedom was never threatened.

Mick: You're so blind. You don't realize you were victims of war profiteers and greedy politicians who ripped you from your normal lives and shipped you off to die for their own gains.

Joe: Isn't that something? Now I'm a victim. Back in my day, they called us heroes.

Mick: It's all a lie, man. There's nothing heroic in war.

Joe: Really? You mean there's nothing heroic in fighting for freedom? Nothing heroic in laying down your life for another?

Mick: Dude, no one had the right to ask you to sacrifice yourself for people half a world away.

Joe: You know, half a world away isn't as far away as it used to be. When I went to war, we saw people struggling to keep the freedoms we have always taken for granted. We knew if they lost their fight, it was only a matter of time before we could lose ours.

Mick: You really believe that old lie? That to defend our freedom we have to fight on foreign soil?

Joe: Kid, I don't know if you realize this but most people in the world don't have the freedoms we do. It's because of people like me, who made the ultimate sacrifice, that you have the right to march in protest.

Mick: That's not true.

Joe: It is true. You think the people of Germany would have been permitted to march against Hitler? Or that the Russians could have marched against Stalin? Do you honestly believe the people of Iraq could march against Hussein? No one marched against their governments because to do so would be suicide. Only in a country like America can you protest against the government. Only in America can you march in protest of the very policies that sustain your right to protest.

Mick: So what do we do? Lay down our signs and go along with whatever stupid stuff the government tells us?

Joe: You do that, and I really did die in vain. Go ahead, have your march. State your case. Stand up for what you believe. But never forget that the freedom of speech and assembly that you have came at a price. A price thousands of your fellow citizens paid in blood.

[Joe starts to leave.]

Mick: Wait.

[Joe stops.]

Mick: Why did you do it? How could you give up your whole life for anyone other than yourself? That's the one thing I will never understand.

Joe: Greater love has no man than this: that he lay down his life for another.

A Mother's Memories

NANCY B. GIBBS

This is a fictional, yet true-to-life story, but similar situations probably occur in every home when a child loses his or her life in combat.

"My son looked so handsome," she may have explained. "When the recruiter's van pulled away from the curb with my son sitting inside, I noticed only one thing. The way my boy turned around and looked at me let me know he wasn't coming home."

The day she received the news, I am certain she wanted to die with him. She would never forget the little boy who wrapped his tiny hand around her pinky a few hours following his birth.

The sound of his laughter would ring in her mind forever. The funny jokes he told would always make her smile.

The remembrance of the tears he shed when his first-grade sweetheart broke his heart would bring tears to her eyes as well.

He thought nothing could be worse than losing his four-legged friend, Max, to cancer. She remembered the funeral in the backyard and the two sticks he wired together to make a cross.

She looked at the toothless grin in the picture that sat on the mantle. She remembered how hard it was to get him to take a bath and wash his hair that day. Following her insistence, he smiled brightly for the camera.

She walked into his bedroom. The door had been closed since the day he left for battle. The bed was made, but dust covered the furniture. It reminded her that he had been away much too long. Tears flowed down her cheeks as reality told her that he would never return.

She picked up the baseball glove and placed her hand inside. His hand once filled the place where her hand now rested. She remembered how excited he became on game day. He didn't sleep well the nights before the games. Winning was so important to him.

She looked under his bed. She picked up his dirty cleats and thought about how his favorite shoes took him around so many bases. His scuffed dress shoes reminded her of how he eagerly got ready on Sunday mornings for Sunday school.

She glanced over at the leather Bible on his dresser. He was so excited to see his name engraved in gold on the outside cover.

Her mind quickly took her to the day her son made a profession of faith and accepted Christ as his Lord and Savior. With that knowledge, she was able to dry away the tears from her own eyes. She knew her son was safe and sound in the arms of God's Son, Jesus Christ.

As the weeks passed, her ability to face another day grew easier. She was finally able to smile when she thought about the little boy who stole her heart the day he was born. She remembered the good times when life was easy and how his joking spirit made her laugh.

Early one morning, she tied together two sticks with a piece of wire and took a cross to his grave site. As she stuck it into the ground, she remembered the words he spoke after they buried Max so many years earlier. "Max is in Heaven now, Mom. And one day I will see him again." She envisioned her son in Heaven playing catch with his dog.

Somehow, she knew that it wouldn't be long before she would see her son again as well. She smiled as a cool breeze caressed her cheeks. She was certain her son had just blown her a great big kiss from Heaven. And it felt so good!

Remember Them

KAREN M. LEET

When you think of them, say a prayer. Name them one by one. Stand at a war memorial, a statue, a grave marker in a cemetery. Bow your head and think of them—so many gone too soon, so many gone too young, so many gone from friends and family. Wives or husbands, children, moms and dads, brothers and sisters left behind. All their hopes and dreams, their plans for tomorrow, their high expectations—gone, left behind. All that might have been—left behind.

There might be some you knew—a name here and there, a face you recall, a familiar voice, a laugh you used to hear. Long gone. They might include a loved one of your own. Or they might be strangers. Think of them and how they served and gave all they could give—for us, for our safety and freedom, for our nation, for our future.

When you think of them, say a prayer. Thank God for them, for their lives. Thank God on this special day set aside for remembering them, for appreciating them, for honoring their sacrifice. Thank God for each and every one. Name them one by one. At war memorials. At statues. At grave markers in cemeteries. Wherever you go, think of them and say a prayer for them.

Remember them—the men and women who died in service to their country.

Remember them—this day and every day.

Remember them and when you think of them, say a prayer for each and every one.

Remember them.

Memorial Day Poems

HEROES

LOIS ROTZ

Fallen comrades, heroes great
heard stern duty's call.
They bravely sacrificed their lives.
In battle they did fall.

They weren't afraid to face the foe
to gain the victory
and make this world a safer place
for people just like me.

Today we offer heartfelt thanks,
remembering those who died
protecting this great country.
We honor them with pride.

HAIL

DOLORES STEGER

Hail those who throughout history
have served our country steadfastly.
For bravery and faith they stand
as symbols of a righteous land.
Great praise is given them today,
defenders of the USA.

IN MEMORY

DOLORES STEGER

From earthly realms they've been set free;
they're now a part of history.
Yet living on in memory,
they're heroes, justifiably.

Father's Memories

BETSEY MCKEE

Summary: A father recalls the different stages of his daughters' and sons' lives as he looks through a photo album.

Characters:

Father
Mother
Baby
Child—4- or 5-year-old male or female
Boy—9 or 10 years old
Teen Girl
Teen Boy
Older Teen Girl as Bride

Setting: living room
Props: living room chair, rocking chair, photo album, blanket, pillow, teddy bear, pajamas, play clothes, baseball and glove, fad clothing, suitcase, jeans, bride dress, bouquet, doll if real baby is not used, camera to flash for each character's appearance
Running Time: 7 minutes

Father is seated front stage left in living room chair, looking at photo album. (Except for Father, characters will enter stage right, remain motionless center stage and exit stage left.) Mother is seated in rocking chair, motionless, looking down at Baby wrapped in blanket. Camera flashes.

Father: It seems like only yesterday when you were born. I felt so inadequate, but already I loved you so much. *[sweetly, looking at baby and mother]* You are Daddy's little princess. I won't let anyone hurt you.

[Mother with Baby exits. Father turns more pages. Child in pajamas enters, carrying a pillow and teddy bear, places head on pillow, eyes closed. Camera flashes.]

Father: You grew so quickly and the years slipped through my fingers. I hoped you wouldn't grow so fast. *[sternly, but not mean]* You've already had six drinks of water, six kisses, and been to the bathroom a hundred times, and I tucked you in and scared away the monster 25 times—now go to bed! *[softens voice]* I love you too.

[Child exits. Father turns pages. Boy in play clothes enters, with a baseball and glove. He looks up, head slightly to the side. Camera flashes.]

Father: I wanted to keep you with me always and you felt the same. I still remember the day you said, "I don't want to grow up." When I asked why, you said, "Because I don't want to leave you and Mommy." The love you had for us melted my heart. *[pauses]* Sure, I'll play ball with you, but let me finish this first. *[more softly to himself]* I never seemed to finish, though.

[Boy exits. TEEN GIRL dressed in fad casual clothing enters, arms folded, looking disgusted. Camera flashes.]

Father: There were times when you asserted your independence, and I wasn't sure if either of us would survive. *[angrily and loud]* You are not going anywhere dressed like that! I don't care if everyone else is doing it! Don't you talk to me like that! Fine, you're grounded . . . don't you slam that door! *[sound of slamming door]*

[TEEN GIRL exits. Father turns pages slowly. Teen Boy in jeans enters, carrying suitcase, sets suitcase down, and waves good-bye. Camera flashes.]

Father: Then you were gone—off to college. You seemed too young for us to leave you there by yourself. As I hugged you and walked away, I felt like someone was tearing out my heart, but I knew this was best. I could barely see driving home as the tears filled my eyes. *[lecturing tone]* Now remember—Stay away from drugs and alcohol. Don't forget what we taught you. Be sure to find a good church and Christian friends. Make sure you eat right. Don't forget why you're here. Be sure to be in by midnight. And, uh, could you call us and write once in awhile? *[pauses]* I love you.

[Teen Boy exits. Older Teen Girl as Bride in bride dress enters, carrying bouquet and smiling. Father turns pages, stops and looks straight ahead. Camera flashes.]

Father: The day came when you got married. I was no longer "the man" in your life and that hurt a little, but I knew this new man would take care of you and love you as I still do. If not, he would answer to me. Walking down the aisle and giving you away was one of the hardest things I ever had to do. *[speaks softly to Older Teen Girl as Bride]* Don't forget old Dad, OK? *[Older Teen Girl as Bride exits. Father turns another page, wipes away a tear. Father is left alone on stage. He flips pages quickly and then stops.]*

Father: *[as if reflecting]* How quickly the years passed as though they had wings. From the moment all of you were born, I was constantly saying good-bye as you began that journey of separation from your mother and me, but none of you ever left my heart and hopefully I will never leave yours. *[pauses and looks up to the front as though his children were before him]* I love you, son. I love you, daughter. *[bows head]* Dear Lord, thank You for my children. I'm so glad that they know You as their Savior. I know, Lord, that I can put them in Your hands even though they are no longer in mine because You care for them. As Your Word says, "Train a child in the way he should go, and when he is old he will not turn from it" *[Proverbs 22:6]*. Amen.

[FATHER stands, places photo album on chair, and exits.]

Father Knows Best

DOUGLAS RAYMOND ROSE

Narrator: Attention all you fathers.
Today we honor you.
We thank you for your work and care.
Happy Father's Day to you!

[Dad and baby walk across stage.]

Narrator: Thanks, Dad, for helping us babies
and tickling us under the chin.
You helped Mom change our diapers
and said, "You're Daddy's little man."

[Dad and toddler walk together across stage.]

Narrator: As toddlers we waited for you to come home.
We'd meet you at the door,
wanting you to come play with us
and wrestle all over the floor.

[Dad with preschooler holding his hand walk across stage.]

Narrator: As preschoolers we loved to imitate you,
trying to walk in your big shoes.
We tried to take steps just like yours
and stick to you like glue.

[Dad and boy with schoolbooks walk across stage.

Narrator: The day came when to school we went.
We tried hard to be big and brave.
We wanted Dad to be proud of us,
so we gave you a big smile and wave.

[Dad with junior age boy flexing muscles walk across stage.]

Narrator: As junior boys we increased in stature.
We wanted muscles just like Dad.
We drank our milk and ate our peas
to get the super strength Dad had.

[Dad and teenage son walk across stage.]

Narrator: Now I'm a high school senior.
Dad has some great ideas for me too.
It's surprising how much my dad's learned
since I first started school!

[Young dad walks across stage holding new son.]

Narrator: Now I no longer go to school.
I'm happily married and I'm glad.
A wonderful change has taken place.
I'm the guy my own son will call "dad."

So, Fathers, no matter what your age,
we sons need your prayers and patience too;
we'll never outgrow your great influence,
so, Happy Father's Day, Dad to you!

Father's Day Poems

MY DAD

AMY HOUTS

Daddy is my special friend
on whose love I can depend.
Daddy is my hero, strong.
Daddy, you can do no wrong.
I love you, Dad, and I can say
just how much on Father's Day!

YOU ARE

DOLORES STEGER

You are goodness, you are strength,
an inspiration, it is true.
That's why I thank our God above
for bringing me to you.

TO DAD, WITH LOVE

LORENA WORLEIN

When I look back on memories
I treasure in my heart,
there are so many special ones
in which you played a part.
You always seemed to know each time
that I would have some needs,
and you were always there to help
with words or kindly deeds.

You set me an example, Dad,
on how to live each day.
You taught me to have faith in God
and showed me how to pray.
You told me I could count on Him
whatever might betide,
no matter what might happen
He'd be there at my side.

When you saw me struggle
you'd lend a guiding hand,
and when you saw me falter,
you'd gently help me stand.
The lessons I have learned from you
have helped me every day.
Your wisdom and your guidance
have led me in God's way.

I can't begin to tell you
how much you mean to me.
I am extremely grateful
and proud as I can be.
Somehow a simple "thank you"
would never, ever do,
for words alone can not express
the love I have for you.

FATHER'S DAY DIARY

DOUGLAS RAYMOND ROSE

It's time to clean out childhood things
here in our empty nest.
After all, the kids are grown.
Why save this childish mess?

As I packed the games in boxes,
my memory chip clicked in.
I thought of all the games Junior
played with his favorite leather
catcher's mitt.

Daughter's dolls were many
in a row, parading across the floor.
I put some in a big trash bag
and then went back for more.

But—no—I couldn't do it!
I'll clean this room another day.
For now I'll store these treasured toys
and for grandchildren I'll patiently
pray.

DAD'S GREATEST JOB
(BASED ON PROVERBS 1:8)

DOUGLAS RAYMOND ROSE

Training children is the world's
highest calling.
Cultivating them well is God's plan.
The most fragrant flowers grow not
wild.
It takes a deeply dedicated hand.
Bring out the best in your offspring.
Help them personally pursue God's
plan.
Dad's greatest job is training children.
So let Father God lend you a hand!

A QUIVER FULL

L. RUTH CARTER

The tears of a small child chased away
by the sunshine of your smile.
The gloom dispelled on a rainy day
by your time to play a while.
The sorrows and pains of a teen
made small by your sympathy.
The insecure and in-between
made big by your empathy.

The grace you pour out to everyone
reflects our Savior's love.
Your giving to both daughters and
sons
directs us to God above.
May we never take for granted
your love, oh, mom and dad.
Instead in all our hearts be planted
active faith that makes you glad.

DAD'S GREATEST GIFT

DOUGLAS RAYMOND ROSE

I love the gifts you gave me,
from cards to ceramic vases;
it thrilled me no end to see
your happy, smiling faces.

But though you've given much to me
that I lovingly today recall.
You've grown up to be an awesome
adult—
that's my greatest gift of them all!

SPECIAL

DOLORES STEGER

You make the world more special
just by being there.
Your love and trust and confidence
show me how much you care.
You set a good example
in everything you do.
That's why, Dad, it's my greatest hope
I'll grow to be like you.

Printing the Truth

JORLYN A. GRASSER

Summary: Mr. Zenger daily printed the truth in his newspaper in spite of threats to his life. In time, these brave acts led to Mr. Zenger's imprisonment. Andrew Hamilton, the famous lawyer, unexpectedly appeared to defend him. The truth won out and Mr. Zenger went free.

Characters: If enough people are available, the speakers' roles will not have to double up. Speakers are also men or women waiting for newspapers. All men and boys wear knee-length breeches and women and girls wear long dresses or skirts.

Narrator
Mr. Zenger
John Zenger—boy, age 11
Pieter Zenger—boy, age 9
Speaker 1 and/or Court Clerk
Speaker 2 and/or Neighbor
Speaker 3 and/or Jury Foremen
Speaker 4 and/or Soldier (wearing uniform)
Mrs. Zenger
Andrew Hamilton (wearing top hat and suit)

Setting: November 1733, a small print shop/kitchen stage right with a divider between them, and a speaker stand on the left

Props: mural of printing press, table, newspapers with "The New York Weekly Journal, November 29, 1733" at top, dishes, mixing bowl, spoon, speaker stand, stool

Running Time: 20 minutes

Narrator: Our nation's struggle for freedom began with major battles, but continued in towns and villages one brave person at a time. Peter Zenger was such a person. His sons, John and Pieter, helped their father with the printing press.

[Men and women gather front stage right.]

John: Come help me fold these printed pages, Pieter. Then we can deliver them to the people waiting outside.

[Both fold newspapers, then give to men and women.]

Narrator: The boys handed out the newspapers to the waiting people. John glanced at the date on the paper: November 29, 1733. The *New York Weekly Journal* had been printed only a few weeks now and already it was a huge success. The boys listened as those standing nearby began to discuss the news.

Speaker 1: Read what it says about Governor Cosby. He is spending our money to buy fancy clothes and a big piece of land.

Speaker 2: It says Governor Cosby will not allow anyone to work in a government office if he does not do exactly as the governor wishes.

Speaker 3: Oh, how terrible! The governor nearly killed a small child and a farmer as they were walking along the road. His carriage hit them, and he rushed right on by.

Speaker 4: This printer may be punished and even hanged for printing these things about the governor, even if it is true.

[John steps back, afraid, while Pieter and Speakers exit.]

Narrator: That last statement made John's heart freeze. Will Governor Cosby do harm to his father? He must talk to his mother about that.

[John moves to table and Mrs. Zenger joins him.]

Mrs. Zenger: *[talking to John as she stirs a mixing bowl]* Yes, your father is taking a risk in printing about the wrongs of Governor Cosby. But if he did not do it, the people would have no way of knowing the truth. You must do all you can to help your father.

[Both exit.]

Narrator: A year went by very quickly. The governor, who could not read very well, had his advisors take care of his business. It took some time before he realized the *New York Weekly Journal* was exposing him. It was a lazy Sunday afternoon. The Zenger family had attended a long church service and was now preparing for lunch.

[John, Pieter, and Mrs. Zenger enter kitchen. Mr. Zenger is in pressroom.]

Pieter: I'm hungry. Let me help set the table. *[gathers dishes and places on table]*

Mrs. Zenger: It will just be a few minutes. John, go call your father.

[Soldiers enter pressroom to arrest Mr. Zenger.]

Narrator: John stopped near the doorway when he heard angry voices.

[John stands center stage—action left stage.]

Mr. Zenger: *[pleading]* Let me say goodbye to my wife and children!

Soldier: *[roughly]* No, you need to come with me now!

Narrator: John realized his father was in trouble and ran to get his mother. They both returned in time to see Mr. Zenger being dragged away.

[Soldier takes Mr. Zenger down aisle.]

Mrs. Zenger: *[hysterical]* My husband! They are taking my husband to jail! *[collapses to floor, crying]*

Narrator: John could feel hot tears in his eyes. He must help, but what could he do? Mr. Zenger remained in jail for nine months. During that time, John helped his mother run the paper and continued to print the wrongdoings of Governor Cosby. On August 4, 1735, Peter Zenger was tried. *[All actors gather on stage left.]* People gathered from miles around. As the meeting was about to begin, a disturbance at the back door of the courthouse caused a stir. A distinguished man entered the room.

Pieter: What's happening? All I can see is someone with a black hat moving toward the front.

Mrs. Zenger: It's Andrew Hamilton, the famous lawyer. He has come to defend Father.

Narrator: A hush fell over the entire crowd as Andrew Hamilton began to speak.

[Andrew Hamilton stands on stool.]

Andrew Hamilton: *[in solemn, deep voice]* The question before the court and you, gentlemen of the jury, is not the cause of the poor printer nor of New York alone. What the jury will decide today is not whether one printer can print the truth, but whether all people have the right to print and read the truth. It may in its consequences affect every free man in America. It is the best cause. It is the cause of liberty.

[Everyone applauds, then moves about in small groups talking among themselves.]

Narrator: The trial ended. Now the rest was up to the jury.

[Pieter and John move away from the crowd.]

Pieter: What do you think the jury will decide?

John: Father is not guilty of printing lies. If they are honest men, the jury will free him.

Neighbor: *[shouts]* Wait! The jury is back!

John: They were only gone about ten minutes. Let's hurry.

[Both boys move back to left stage.]

Narrator: The large crowd had returned, buzzing with excitement. Would Mr. Zenger be free?

Court Clerk: Quiet everyone. *[turning to the jury foreman]* What is the jury's verdict?

Foreman: *[shouts]* Not guilty!

Narrator: A large cheer arose from the crowd. Mr. Zenger was free. He could continue to print the truth. John and Pieter joined the crowd. They all eagerly congratulated Andrew Hamilton and Mr. Zenger.

Everyone: Hurrah! Hurrah! *[They congratulate each other and shake hands as they walk offstage.]*

God Bless America

KAREN M. LEET

You've seen the bumper stickers, right? They come in a variety of shapes and sizes. They say "God bless America." And especially in times of trial and trouble, in times of shock and suffering, in times of strain and threat, that's our cry, that's our prayer.

God, we pray, bless our country—bless America and keep her safe. Watch over her and guard her, protect and guide her, cover her with Your wings and set Your angels to stand by her, our nation, our America.

On days set aside to honor our land and remember how we started, we fly our flags and wear our colors—the red, white, and blue. We hold picnics and parades. We enjoy concerts and cookouts. We celebrate our history in a dozen ways. Best of all we fill the skies with bursts of bright fireworks and we hear the great booms as they explode overhead. We *ooh* and *aah* and applaud. And that's all good.

We love our country. We enjoy wonderful rights and privileges. Our land is wide and varied, brimming over with abundances—abundances of lakes and rivers, plains and mountains, farms and cities, parks and resources. We are richly blessed here in America, and so it's good and right for us to celebrate.

And it's good and right for us to gather in worship and prayer. We have, as a nation, so much to be grateful for, so much to appreciate and enjoy, so much to thank our God for giving us. Really, if you think about it, God has blessed and is blessing America. He has poured out great and wonderful blessings on us and on our nation.

So when we see those bumper stickers on cars and trucks that say, "God bless America," perhaps—just perhaps—we could add another bumper sticker too. One that says, "America, bless God."

We've been richly blessed by God and have been given a nation well worth celebrating. Let's never forget how greatly He has already blessed us—let's never forget to say thank You, God—let's never forget, as individuals, as believers, as Americans to bless Him in return.

So, let's say it, yes—God bless America—and yes, America, never ever forget to bless God.

Prayer for Independence Day

EVA JULIUSON

I could easily have been born in another country. I am greatly blessed to have been born in America. Not too many countries have had so many people willing to lay down their lives for the sake of others' freedom. Father, remind me to never take freedom for granted. I am still free to write or speak out about what I agree or disagree with. I am still free to choose my leaders. I am still free to work where I want, have as many kids as I want, shop where I want, worship at the church of my choice, go to church at all, have a prayer or Bible study group in my home, tell of my beliefs.

Even as I pray, I know there are those in other countries who are imprisoned for holding church in their homes, for having a Bible, for speaking against the government, for not bowing down to the gods of man. There are those in other countries who do not have access to schools or healthcare or work or food or fresh water. There are those who are not allowed any kind of rights because of their gender or race.

On this birthday of America, I thank You for giving our forefathers the vision of a self-governing people who could freely give glory and honor to You. Forgive us, Lord, when we use our freedom to rebel or ignore You. Forgive us our sinful haughtiness.

Thank You for the thousands since our country's birth who have been willing to die for my freedom. America's freedom could be taken away if not careful. Thank You most of all for Jesus' willingness to die for my eternal freedom—the kind that can never be taken away! In Jesus' name, amen.

Independence Day Poems

GRAND CELEBRATION

SUSAN SUNDWALL

High waves the flag
over people and nation,
a red, white, and blue
grand celebration.

Remembering the freedom
hard fought for and won
by the valiant and brave
for each daughter and son.

Sweet Liberty's song
rang joyous and clear
defying oppressor
and beating back fear.

Deep in the battle
from hillside to sea
they kept close to God
so we could be free.

With each step you take
on the soil of our nation
recall what it took
to secure its creation.

Go—send up your rockets
and midst the red glare
pray God that our freedom
will always be there.

BLESSED IS THE NATION

LORENA E. WORLEIN

Blessed is the nation
whose trust is in the Lord,
that seeks to do his will
as found within his Word.
Blessed are the people
God chooses for His own,
who call upon His name
and worship Him alone.

Blessed is the nation
that looks to God in prayer
and glorifies the Lord—
none other can compare.
That nation shall be great
that seeks to do what's right,
obeys all God's commands
and journeys in His light.

Blessed is the nation
that helps all those in need.
That nation, under God,
is very blessed indeed.
Lift up the holy name
of our great God on high
who reigns in majesty
over earth and sea and sky.

GOD'S PRAYER FOR AMERICA

(BASED ON 2 CHRONICLES 7:14)

DOUGLAS RAYMOND ROSE

I love your land, America.
I want to heal your deep wounds today.
I will go before you and protect you,
if my people will humble themselves and pray.

I love your land and citizens.
For your souls a great price I've paid.
My will is that your leaders follow my word and my people will turn from their wicked ways.

I love your people, America.
I love every creed, color, and race.
I desire to forgive your sins and selfish whims, if my people will repent and seek my face.

I love your families and cherished children.
For your marriages and morals I passionately pray.
It's to me, not the voters or politicians, you will give account when you stand before me on Judgment Day.

WE'RE ONE

LOIS ROTZ

One nation under God,
let this our motto be.
One in hope, one in love,
and one in liberty.

One in purpose, one in strength,
standing firm each hour.
Trusting God, we then will see
the glory of His power.

WAVE A FLAG

DOLORES STEGER

Wave a flag for justice,
wave for liberty.
Wave a flag for freedom,
wave so all may see.

Wave a flag for honor,
wave a flag for peace.
Wave for all God's blessings,
wave they never cease.

Wave a flag; keep waving.
Wave to show it's true.
Wave a flag and praise then
our own red, white, and blue.

Sunday Morning Mayhem

JODY INGALLS

Summary: A family takes a look at its motivations for going to Sunday school.

Characters:

Bill—a father trying to get his family to Sunday school
Nancy—an uptight mother
Laura—teenage daughter
Tim—teenage son

Setting: family living room, family car. One side of the stage is set with four chairs which represent the family car. The chairs are arranged in two rows, which are both turned at a 45-degree angle from the audience. The other side of the stage represents the family living room.

Props: laundry basket containing clothes and a curling iron, Bible, 4 chairs, CD of worship songs
Costumes: Sunday morning church attire
Running Time: 7 minutes

Sketch begins with Nancy and Laura and Tim rushing on and off the living room stage, one at a time, frantically getting ready for church: trying to find Bible, socks, curling iron, etc. When Nancy, Laura, and Tim are out of sight, Bill enters, checking watch. He calls offstage.

Bill: Kids! We're going to be late again! You know what our Sunday school teachers said about that! They can't have people just walking in 10 or 20 minutes after class is supposed to start.

Nancy: *[entering stage, busy with getting ready]* Then why don't they start class on time?

Bill: Because nobody is there on time!

Nancy: Well, you've got a point there; but we don't really want to be there early if no one else is, do we? There's always that uncomfortable silence if too few people are in the room.

Bill: *[dryly]* Well, I don't think we're in too much danger of being early. Besides, we could be the ones to set a new trend. Not if the kids don't get here, though. Where are they, anyway?

Nancy: Tim is trying to find his Bible, and Laura is in the bathroom.

Bill: Still? Good grief! It wasn't enough that we got her her own phone line; now we'll have to build her her own addition! Why don't they just get up earlier?

Nancy: Well, it is harder now that we're trying to go to Sunday school. We all have been used to sleeping in. . . . Sounds kind of nice right now.

Bill: Hey! Don't you think we should go to Sunday school?

Nancy: *[unconvinced]* Of course I do. It's a great way to fellowship with new people and get involved.

Bill: Exactly. *[Kids enter in a rush.]* Guys, it's about time! Let's get in the car!

[Characters mime piling in the car. They freeze and, one by one, come to life and reveal their thoughts.]

Laura: I'm so glad we're going to Sunday school now. I hope we're not too late. Of course, I wouldn't mind being just a little late so everyone has a chance to notice my new outfit. I hope that cute guy is there again. I'm sure he kept looking at me during class last week. Megan acts like she owns him, but I don't think she'll be much competition now that I'm part of the inner Sunday school group.

Tim: Sunday school! Whose idea was this anyway? As if I don't get enough school during the week. Sleeping in was way better. I don't know how I'm going to make it through the service with this sleep deprivation. Plus, I'll already have lower resistance to sleep from sitting through the Sunday school lesson. I'm doomed!

Nancy: *[with growing paranoia]* Oh, dear. Here we go again. I don't think I can do this. I hate walking into that room of people where everyone else knows each other! Last week, I'm sure everyone stared at us for the first five minutes. I couldn't even concentrate. The teacher will probably call on me to read today. Just like my junior high class when the name Mephibosheth popped up when it was my turn to read! Then there was the time I squirted jelly donut down my shirt during my college and career class—right in front of my new heartthrob. I don't even remember who he was, but I can still feel the embarrassment! Why do they serve those things at church anyway? They're just saturated fat! Oh, I wish we'd stayed home!

Bill: Ah, another successful launch. I love Sunday mornings. Another chance to further my knowledge. Another chance to further the knowledge of those around me. Sunday school is such a great opportunity to show and use what I've learned. I'm sure I noticed a gleam of respect in the teacher's eye last week. And who could blame him? It's not everyone who is as well versed in Scripture as I am. *[Everyone unfreezes as Bill pauses and speaks his next line]* Hey, it's a little quiet in here. How about some music?

[The radio starts playing a reflective worship song, such as "As the Deer." The family listens in silence. As the music fades, their attitudes change.]

Bill: You know, everyone, that's what this getting up early to go to worship services is all about. I'm afraid I lost sight of why we should go to Sunday school. I'm sorry.

Laura: You're right, Dad. I let other things crowd out any desire to know God better.

Tim: I guess if I think of it that way, rearranging my schedule isn't so bad. I do think they could work a naptime into Sunday morning, though.

Nancy: I think I've been the worst of all. All I've been thinking about is myself. Maybe going to Sunday school will help change all that. What is our class about anyway, honey? I don't think I even noticed last week.

Bill: Well, it looks like we're here. Why don't we go in and find out? If we hurry, there might even be some jelly donuts left. *[winks at his wife as they mime getting out of the car]*

Nancy: *[looking startled]* That was you? How could I have forgotten? Well, I guess that Sunday school experience turned out pretty well, after all. Maybe this one will too! But I am not eating a jelly donut!

Unearned Promotions

JOHN COSPER

Summary: Bruce is surprised when he learns what really happens on Promotion Sunday.

Characters:

Bruce and Katie—Sunday school kids (can be played by kids or adults)

Bruce enters in a kid's suit with a clip-on tie. He stops to check himself in an imaginary mirror.

Bruce: OK, one last check. Coat is straight. Shirt tucked in. Tie is— *[Bruce adjusts his tie. It's a clip-on, and it comes off in his hand. He puts it back on and straightens it.]* Tie is straight. Hair looks good. Today's a big day, buddy. Don't want to mess this up.

[Katie enters.]

Katie: Hi-ya, Bruce.

Bruce: Oh, hello, Katie.

Katie: What are ya doin'?

Bruce: Just getting ready for my big day. Are you here to congratulate me?

Katie: Congratulate you for what?

Bruce: Didn't you hear? It's Promotion Sunday. And I think I have a pretty good idea who's getting promoted in our Sunday school class.

Katie: Who?

Bruce: Well, me, of course!

Katie: You don't think I'll get promoted?

Bruce: Ha-ha, ha-ha! Don't make me laugh.

Katie: Why not?

Bruce: Promotions are for the best. That's what my dad tells me. And he should know. He promotes people every week.

Katie: What's his job?

Bruce: He's a concert promoter.

Katie: So what did you do to earn your promotion?

Bruce: Well, let's see. I had all the books of the Bible memorized before anyone else. I had perfect attendance and a perfect record with Bible memory verses. And I think we all know that my artwork of Jesus rising from the dead on Easter was a work of art.

Katie: What about mine?

Bruce: You colored Jesus pink! Everyone knows that His skin was olive!

Katie: Jesus was green?

Bruce: Face it, this promotion is all mine.

Katie: No way! I heard it was for everybody.

Bruce: Who told you that?

Katie: The teacher! She said everybody gets promoted on Promotion Sunday.

Bruce: We do?

Katie: Everybody who is old enough gets moved up to the next Sunday school group.

Bruce: Everybody?

Katie: Everybody!

Bruce: Wow. I didn't know that's what they meant by Promotion Sunday. I thought it was for the best and the brightest.

Katie: You silly head! Jesus wants us all to grow closer to Him. That's why we all get promoted, regardless of how much we know or how cool we think we are. "The last shall be first, and the first shall be last."

Bruce: Where'd you learn that?

Katie: Sunday school!

Bruce: Well, congratulations on getting promoted.

Katie: Congratulations to you too.

Bruce: And even though we're all getting promoted, I think we should ask for a raise.

Katie: What kind of a raise do you want?

Bruce: I was planning on asking for four cookies at cookie and juice time. But I'll settle for three.

Katie: Sounds good to me!

Promotion Sunday Poems

READY FOR PROMOTION DAY

CHARLOTTE ADELSPERGER

I'm thankful for Sunday school
with lessons from God's Word.
I've experienced how His love
through teachers is transferred.
Learning is like hiking on a path.
New wonders get my attention.
As I grow in knowing Jesus,
each day has a new dimension.
Now promoted to the next class,
I want to learn truths that are key.
When I pray, I believe Christ
is calling, "Come, follow Me."

ETERNAL TEACHERS

(BASED ON 2 CHRONICLES 7:14)

DOUGLAS RAYMOND ROSE

Learn to live and love to learn
helping children reach the top;
teaching influences all of eternity
never telling where their influence
stops.

What better gift can we give children
than teaching them the grace of God?
Teachers influence all of eternity.
Even in Heaven their influence never
stops.

A PROMOTIONAL DAY BLESSING

DOUGLAS RAYMOND ROSE

God bless the boys and bless the girls
on this very special awards day.
It's Promotion Sunday once again.
On all of you His blessings we pray.

Bless the teachers and the parents.
Bless all that the students have learned.
Bless them as they onward go—
with these certificates they have
earned.

Grumbly Hateful or Humbly Grateful?

SUSAN SUNDWALL

Summary: How one ungrateful family learned to be thankful.

Characters:

Dad	Grandma	Child 6
Mom	Child 1	Child 7
Lydia	Child 2	Child 8
Leah	Child 3	Child 9
Levi	Child 4	Child 10
Grandpa	Child 5	Child 11

Setting: It is the night before Thanksgiving. The family is rushing around the house performing last minute preparations.
Props: grocery sacks, kitchen table with Thanksgiving turkey and trimmings
Running Time: 10 minutes

Scene 1

Mom: *[on phone]* OK, Dad, then we'll see you and Mom for lunch. What's that? *[pauses as if listening]* We'll meet Uncle Charlie and Aunt Evelyn later in the afternoon. That sounds good to me. I better get my chores done. Goodbye.

Leah: *[overhears]* Oh, Mom, how can we handle another holiday with them? Uncle Charlie is so annoying and Aunt Evelyn has the most irritating giggle!

Levi: She makes me laugh when she starts laughing so hard and then snorts.

Leah: It sounds like a baby pig. *[snorts]*

Lydia: *[enters sobbing]* Oh, I can't believe it!

Mom: Lydia, what's wrong?

[Lydia attempts to explain, but sobs uncontrollably and cannot be understood.]

Leah: I think I know what's wrong. Her boyfriend broke up with her.

[Mom puts her arms around her just as Dad appears with arms full of groceries.]

Dad: Sorry I'm running so late.

Mom: *[looks at watch]* We have so little time to get everything done and then hurry off to the Thanksgiving service.

Dad: Well, you all were complaining about how cold the house is so I stopped by and got a few parts for the furnace. *[points to Mom]* It cost more than I expected. I think we broke the bank.

Mom: You mean you've got to fix the furnace before we can go to the Thanksgiving service?

Dad: Well, we don't want anybody to catch pneumonia, now do we? *[exits]*

Mom: Come on, kids! You've got to help me put these groceries away so we can get to the Thanksgiving service. I can't believe your father is going to make us late.

[Levi accidentally spills something while putting away groceries.]

Leah: Levi! You just made a huge mess over our clean kitchen. All my hours of cleaning have now gone down the drain just like that! *[snaps fingers]*

Lydia: *[still whimpering]* Do you think I look fat or ugly or stupid? Wait! Don't answer that. *[flees from room]*

Leah: I don't see how we can go to church tonight. We are so . . . so . . . dysfunctional!

Levi: Aww . . . you girls are so emotional. You both get the award for being drama queens. I think our family puts the "fun" in dysfunction.

Mom: If ever I needed to go to church, it's now! Last one in the car is a rotten egg.

Scene 2

Family sits in a pew stage left. They are whispering to each other before service starts.

Mom: *[sarcastically]* It sure feels nice and warm in here.

Dad: When people feel loved and appreciated, a room is warmer.

Leah: Barbie Holzer never even said hi to me tonight. I knew we shouldn't have come.

Lydia: Oh, I'll never be thankful another day in my life.

Levi: Shhhh! Be quiet! It's about to start.

[A group of eleven students form a single line center stage.]

Child 1: I'm thankful for my heritage—the roots from which I came.
May I never do anything that would dishonor my family's name.

Child 2: Thank You, God, for health. Without it we'd be lost.
Help us comfort the sick, no matter what the cost.

Child 3: We sure need communities with citizens who obey the law.
We pray for godly leaders, who keep us proud and standing tall.

Child 4: We have comfortable homes, which we're thankful for.
May they be a haven of love from the ceiling to the floor.

Child 5: For the gifts God has given us, we are blessed beyond measure.

May we always realize our family is our greatest treasure.

Child 6: Thank You, God, for teachers, who are so very smart.
And for the wisdom they daily do impart.

Child 7: I'm thankful for my friends old and new.
Without them I don't know what I'd do.

Child 8: I'm thankful for the gift of God's only Son.
His precious blood brought salvation to everyone.

Child 9: I'm thankful for each trial, though it brings me to my knees.
God has always been faithful and proven His love to me.

Child 10: May God supply all your need—that's what the Scriptures say.
I'm thankful for provisions and mercy He gives to me each day.

Child 11: I am so thankful for God's Word—on it I can trust.
To experience courage, hope, and love daily is a must.

Scene 3

At Thanksgiving table the next day. Attitudes have changed.

Leah: Mom, this looks delicious.

Mom: Thank you, Leah. Everyone pitched in and this has helped make our Thanksgiving the best ever.

Dad: I'm ready for some of my favorite banana cream pie.

Grandma: I wanted to tell each one of you how thankful I am for you. I feel so blessed to have such a loving family.

Lydia: I think the Lord has changed our hearts from being grumbly hateful to humbly grateful.

Grandpa: Really? What happened?

Mom: Last evening at the Thanksgiving program we were encouraged to count our blessings.

Dad: We went into that service thinking one way, but came home thinking completely differently. We realized that we have Jesus, and we have each other.

Mom: And our house may not be warm, but our hearts can be.

Levi: Hey! I got the wishbone.

Leah: Well, Levi, let's hear you make a wish.

Levi: *[shuts eyes]* I wish we could be humbly grateful and never grumbly hateful ever again.

Everyone: *[in unison]* Happy Thanksgiving, everyone!

Money Talks

DIANNE MCINTOSH

Summary: Abe and Ben discover that a meager offering from a special Thanksgiving Day collection has the ability to tell them a great deal about those who give.

Characters:

Ben—Christian man

Abe—Christian man with a unique way of looking at things

Setting: church office or foyer
Props: few dollar bills, wallet with large twenty and fifty dollar bills in it
Running Time: 4 minutes

Abe is holding a small handful of money up to his ear. He has a puzzled expression on his face. Ben approaches with an equally puzzled look on his face.

Ben: What are you doing with that money?

Abe: I'm listening to it.

Ben: *[incredulously]* What?

Abe: It's trying to tell me something.

Ben: *[concerned]* Are you feeling all right?

Abe: *[waves hand at Ben]* Shhh . . . listen. Can you hear its message?

Ben: Um . . . no. No, can't say that I do. *[starts to leave]* I think I'll just mosey along. See you, Abe.

Abe: Stop! You've got to hear this. Listen!

Ben: Really now, money doesn't talk. It's just a little, flat piece of paper.

Abe: Oh, is it now? Just a flat piece of paper. Is that so?

Ben: *[confidently]* Yes, that's so.

Abe: Just a piece of paper?

Ben: Well, it does have value, but it can't talk.

Abe: If it has value, then it can talk.

Ben: How's that?

Abe: It can tell me how far it can go.

Ben: *[gives in]* All right then, what's that money telling you?

Abe: It's telling me it's lonely.

Ben: Oh really, and why would it say that?

Abe: This little bit of money was all that was in the collection plate for the special offering for needy people.

Ben: Really? Those few dollar bills?

Abe: Yeah, pretty pathetic, don't you think? And this was the Thanksgiving Day collection.

Ben: Well, that little bit of money isn't going to go very far.

Abe: That's exactly what the money said.

Ben: *[not listening to Abe]* It sort of says something about us givers too.

Abe: Really? What does it say?

Ben: It says we aren't very thankful to God.

Abe: How can this little bit of money tell you that?

Ben: Have you ever heard about the church in Corinth?

Abe: In the Bible?

Ben: Yes, in the Bible. Well, that church did some real giving and the way the apostle Paul tells it, it's crystal clear that giving and thanksgiving go hand in hand.

Abe: Really? What does it say?

Ben: It explains that in being generous they caused a ripple effect of thanksgiving to be given to God. It says, "This service that you perform is not only supplying the needs of God's people but is also overflowing in many expressions of thanks to God" *[2 Corinthians 9:12]*.

Abe: That's exactly what the money said.

Ben: You know, a thankful heart is a giving heart. It just goes together. I'm filled with thanks to God for all He's done for me and it overflows into giving. So what happened with our Thanksgiving Day offering? Why was it so small?

Abe: Let me ask the money. *[holds money up and talks to it]* Little bit of money, why is this all that was collected?

[Abe puts the money up to his ear and listens, then looks up and smiles uncomfortably.]

Ben: Did the money answer?

Abe: Yes, it did. It told me that my observation that it's small opens the door for me to change its size. I have the ability to cheerfully make it a large offering. If I do, it will help supply the needs of God's people. It will cause an overflowing flood of thankfulness to God.

Ben: It told you to give?

Abe: Yes, generously. It also mentioned you might chip in a little too.

Ben: *[laughs]* Are you sure it said all that?

Abe: If it didn't, God's Word did.

Ben: *[opens wallet and pulls out large bills]* Here, take them.

Abe: Remember, they're just flat pieces of paper.

Ben: I know, but there's value in that paper—value beyond the dollar amount that's printed on it. In fact, giving the money gives me the incredible opportunity to transform it into an expression of thanks to God for His "indescribable gift" to me *[2 Corinthians 9:15]*.

Thanksgiving Poems

I AM THANKFUL!

LORENA E. WORLEIN

I am thankful—deeply thankful—
for your wondrous love for me,
for Your tender care and mercy,
for salvation, full and free.
Your abundance and provision
does supply my every need,
and I could never repay You.
I am truly blessed indeed.

I am grateful—very grateful—
for Your blessings every day,
for direction and for guidance
as I journey on my way.
When my path is filled with danger,
You will hear me when I call.
You will guard my every footstep
lest I falter or I fall.

I am blessed—so very blessed—
when I think of all You've done.
May I never take for granted
all I have in Christ, Your Son.
Fill my heart with thanksgiving
and my lips with grateful praise.
May I humbly bow before You
and adore You all my days.

A PRAYER OF THANKS

LOIS ROTZ

Thanks for love and laughter.
Thanks for bright sunshine.
Thanks for food and family,
and good things that are mine.

Thanks for mom and daddy.
Thanks for all my friends.
Thanks for all Your blessings,
for joys that never end.

I Have Something for You

SHARON LESSMAN

Summary: The pastor of a church is feeling unappreciated by his congregation. Throughout the day members bring him gifts that symbolize their appreciation of him.

Characters:

Pastor Dan—male, any age
Mrs. Gorke—older woman
Justin and Tiffany—young married couple
Henry—older man
Steve—adult male, any age
Trudy—young woman

Setting: A pastor's office with a desk or card table covered with papers. Designate a "door" for the office.

Props: desk or card table, folding chair, papers and books for desk, alarm clock, homemade loaf of bread, green branch, fishing pole, file boxes

Running Time: 5 minutes

Pastor Dan sits at desk praying.

Pastor Dan: Lord, I don't know how much longer I can keep this up. I seem to be falling further and further behind with so many people in crises right now. I hardly have time to write a sermon, let alone clean up my desk. I feel drained, unappreciated, and really tired. Maybe I could take a nap for a few minutes. *[lays head on desk and closes his eyes]*

[Mrs. Gorke knocks several times. Pastor doesn't hear it.]

Mrs. Gorke: Pastor? Pastor Dan, are you in there? You're not taking a nap, are you?

Pastor Dan: *[puts his head up, rubs his eyes]* Please come in, Mrs. Gorke.

Mrs. Gorke: Are you OK? You look a little tired.

Pastor Dan: Yes, I guess I am a bit tired.

Mrs. Gorke: I have something for you. *[hands him a clock]*

Pastor Dan: *[questioningly]* Hmm, it's a clock. Does this mean you think my sermons are too long?

Mrs. Gorke: *[laughing]* No, it's my way of saying thank you for all the time you spent with Ralph and me when he was in the hospital before he passed away. Your presence meant a lot to both of us.

Pastor Dan: I was glad to be there with you both.

[Pastor puts clock on desk while Mrs. Gorke exits. He sits down to go through papers, when he hears a knock.]

Pastor Dan: I wonder who that could be? Looks like I'm not going to make much headway with this paperwork today. Come in.

Tiffany: Good morning, Pastor Dan. We hope we're not disturbing you.

Pastor Dan: Oh no, it's fine. How are you today?

Justin: We're great. Tiffany made bread yesterday, and we thought you might enjoy some. *[hands Pastor loaf of bread]* It made us think about how you feed us God's Word every Sunday in your sermons. Sometimes we get a thick slice and sometimes a thin slice, but we know you put a lot of thought into what you say and we're grateful for that.

Pastor Dan: Thanks, and I'd appreciate your prayers for my messages so we can all continue to grow in faith. *[puts bread on desk and couple leaves]*

[After a minute, Henry knocks and Pastor opens door to let him in. Both men appear uncomfortable.]

Pastor Dan: Henry, what can I do for you?

Henry: *[sticks out a green branch, clears his throat]* Here.

Pastor Dan: What's this . . . an olive branch?

Henry: As close as I could get to one. I know we disagreed the other night and I said some things I shouldn't have. I know you're not perfect. No one is. Will you forgive me?

Pastor Dan: Of course, and I ask for your forgiveness too. After all, we are on the same side. *[shake hands and Henry leaves]*

[Pastor props branch up beside desk. Steve knocks on the door.]

Pastor Dan: The door's open.

[Steve enters with a fishing pole.]

Pastor Dan: Let me guess. You're giving me a fishing pole?

Steve: Well, no, you can't have it, but you can use it. You've been working awfully hard lately, Pastor. How would you like to go fishing with me on Saturday morning? I hear the trout they're pulling in from the lake are quite nice this year.

Pastor Dan: I would love to go fishing, Steve, but I don't know if I can spare the time.

Steve: Oh, come on, it will be good for you.

[Just then Trudy walks in with file boxes.]

Trudy: Hi, Pastor Dan. I came by to see if you needed any help. *[looks around]* Hmm, looks like you could use some organization around here. I'd be glad to come once or twice a week to help you corral all this paperwork if you'd like.

Pastor Dan: *[laughs]* That would be fantastic, Trudy. And Steve, I'd love to go fishing Saturday morning. What time shall we make it?

[Everyone leaves the office. Pastor sits to pray.]

Pastor Dan: Dear Lord, thank You for such a concrete answer to my prayer. Forgive me for getting self-focused and for feeling sorry for myself. Bless all of these dear people for letting me know that they do appreciate my efforts, even when I fall short. Thank You for reminding me that we're all in this together and that it's Your strength that sees us through. Amen.

[Pastor smiles contently and walks out the door, whistling or humming.]

In Appreciation of Our Pastor

Carol S. Redd

Summary: A Pastor Appreciation service allows us to take advantage of an opportunity to lift up and encourage the pastor God sent to shepherd our church. This presentation makes a powerful impact by having multiple presenters and the visual of an increasing number of roses in the vase.

Characters: 16 speakers
Setting: open stage area with microphone in center, table should be placed near microphone so vase is within easy reach of speakers
Props: microphone, table, large vase, greenery placed in vase prior to presentation, ribbon tied around neck of vase, 16 roses
Running Time: 10 minutes

Each speaker walks to the microphone carrying a rose which is placed in the vase after reciting his or her part.

Speaker 1:
We were going to write something funny
because that's usually just our way,
but God didn't give us humorous thoughts,
just some serious things to say.

Speaker 2:
God allowed us to think of Sundays
when away in our cars we had sped.
But we may not have noticed that you stayed back
to minister to someone instead.

Speaker 3:
God allowed us to think of fun family times;
those times with our families were priceless.
But sometimes your family just had to wait
while you helped someone facing a crisis.

Speaker 4:
God allowed us to think of those special plans,
the ones looked to with anticipation.
Though your special plans often had to be changed
as you ministered to this congregation.

Speaker 5:
God allowed us to think of those holidays,
those special days like none other.
But sometimes you had to rearrange yours
to visit a lost sister or brother.

Speaker 6:
You've been such a spiritual example.
You've been our leader, our friend, our guide
as we've watched you present our Savior
in great humility, never personal pride.

Speaker 7:
So how can we ever say thank you
for the example that you have shown?
When there were needs you always responded,
placing those of others before those of your own.

Speaker 8:
And when someone lost one she held precious,
when the pain was just too deep to bear,
you offered her the one great Comforter—
broken hearts He'd begin to repair.

Speaker 9:
When one was frightened and feeling broken
and it was Jesus he needed to find,
you offered him the one true Healer—
wounds He'd gently begin to bind.

Speaker 10:
When someone was feeling frightened,
with no one to call her own,
you offered her an Eternal Friend,
one who would never leave her alone.

Speaker 11:
When someone was lost and wandering
along a road wide in every part,
you directed him to the narrow way,
where the Holy Spirit would fill his heart.

Speaker 12:
When one was burdened by her personal sins
and felt there was no hope in sight,
you offered her our precious Savior
and prayed she would follow His light.

Speaker 13:
When someone had tried every possible way
to free his life from a personal mess,
you introduced him to the Master
and then stood back to watch Him bless.

Speaker 14:
When someone reading Holy Scriptures
didn't understand what was read or preached,
you introduced her to the great Teacher,
who, alone, her heart could reach.

Speaker 15:
So in this Pastor Appreciation Month,
just know in our eyes you stand tall.
You've demonstrated what's most important
and that is being obedient to His call.

Speaker 16:
Now we've told God and we've told one another
and want to be sure that you know it too,
that when we asked God to send us a pastor,
we're so thankful that He sent us you.

I Am the Pastor

Stacey Johnson

I am the pastor.
Some see me as the mouthpiece of God. The peacekeeper. The guardian of the flock.
Many expect me to do miracles. Just last week I was asked to "make" a wayward teen come to the Lord.
Often I am criticized. My hair is getting too long. My wife doesn't do enough. My sermons are too long.
I sometimes feel tired, and I can feel the forces of darkness waging war against me.
You see, I am on the front lines of a great battle.
You often find me in chinos and a button-up shirt, but under it, there is armor for war.
Many times I am wounded in this battle.
Sometimes you help the enemy inflict the wounds without even knowing it.
I wish that you could see beneath the armor.
I am a man.
I have chosen to follow God's plan for my life.
I walk forward, many times into the unknown.
I long for you to see me as I am—not what you want me to be.
I find the greatest joy in leading you when you trust me, pray for me, and accept me.
Together, we are Christ's body.
I need your support as I lead us in the battle.
Let's do this, together.

Pastor Appreciation Poems

To My Pastor

Lois Rotz

You're always spreading sunshine
with your happy, cheerful smile.
We know you're always willing
to go the extra mile.

And so we want to thank you
for the thoughtful things you do.
But most of all we thank you
for simply being you.

WE APPRECIATE YOU, PASTOR

LORENA E. WORLEIN

Some years ago you came to us
along with your dear wife
to work and labor at our church,
to share your heart and life.
You felt this was God's plan for you
that God had called you here
to be our leader and our guide.
His plan for you was clear.

And through the years that you
have been
our pastor and our friend,
we found in you a man of God
on whom we could depend.
And so we come before the Lord
to honor you this day
and ask that God would bless your life.
For this we humbly pray.

GIVE PRAISE

DOLORES STEGER

Give praise for our church and its leaders.
Let them know they are valued by all
and we're thankful that we have them with us.
We're thankful they answered God's call.

EXPRESSIONS OF GRATITUDE

LENORA MCWHORTER

Oftentimes we have neglected
to express our gratitude.
Though we can't help but notice
all the thoughtful things you do.

But today we join our hearts
to say thanks from one and all.
for the services you render
in big ways and in small.

We hold you dear in our hearts
in our thoughts and in our prayers
for your humbleness in service
and for always being there.

We thank you for your faithfulness.
And we thank the Father too
for directing your path daily
and the grace He extends to you.

One day it will be worth it all
when a crown you shall wear
and your reward will be waiting
in that homeland over there.

You will hear the Savior whisper,
"Well done, my child, well done.
You have fought a good fight
and your race was well run."